FUN WITH

Machines and Movement

BARBARA TAYLOR

Kingfisher Books

MACHINES AND MOVEMENT

In this book, you can discover how machines make our lives easier and how forces such as friction and gravity affect movement.

The book is divided into eight different topics. Look out for the big headings with a circle at each end – like the one at the top of this page. These headings tell you where a new topic starts.

What is a Machine?

Simple machines; levers; balancing; mobiles.

Stop and Go

Inertia; seat belts and safety.

Wheels go Round

Shapes of wheels; axles; pulleys; gear wheels.

Look at the objects along the bottom of these two pages. Did you know that they are all simple machines? You probably think of machines as big, noisy, complicated things such as lawnmowers, washing machines or robots. But a machine is any device that makes work easier. A machine usually involves movement.

Scissors make it easier to cut things.
A bicycle makes it easier to go fast.
A screw helps to hold pieces of wood together.
A spade makes it easier to dig the garden.
A crane makes it easier to lift heavy weights.

Lever

Wheel

Slope

Wedge

There are five very simple machines that are the basis of all the other machines we use. They are:

the lever
the wheel
the slope
the wedge
the screw

Screw

Look out for these machines as you read this book. Try making a list of all the machines in your home or school. Which room has the most machines?

Lifting with Levers

A lever is a bar that swings, or pivots on a fixed point called a fulcrum. A lever makes it easier to lift heavy things. Your arm is a kind of lever. So are scissors, spades, pliers, tweezers, brooms, wheelbarrows and see-saws. If you push one end of a lever down, the other end moves up.

Make a lever by balancing a plank of wood over a small block of wood. The block is the fulcrum. Try lifting a brick with your lever. Is it easier to lift the brick if the fulcrum is nearer to the brick or farther away?

There are three kinds of lever. Each one has the pushing force (the effort), the pivot (fulcrum) and the weight (the load) in different places. This allows each of them to do a different job.

A first class lever has the fulcrum between the effort and the load. A second class lever has the load between the effort and the fulcrum. A third class lever has the effort between the fulcrum and the load.

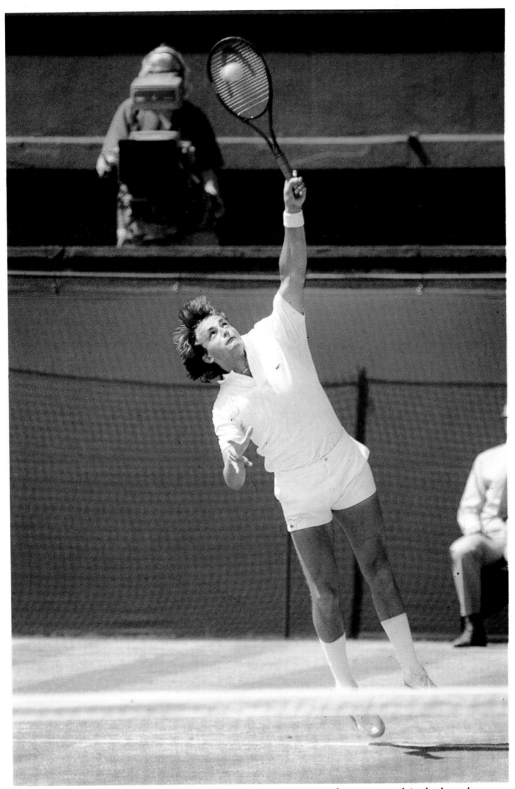

▲ In this picture, the tennis player's arm is working as a third class lever. The effort is the muscles of the upper arm, which are in between the fulcrum (the shoulder) and the load (the ball hitting the racquet).

Balancing

How good are you at balancing?
Put a ball on the floor near a wall.
Stand with your heels right up
against the wall. Now try to pick
up the ball without moving your
feet.

It's impossible! When you bend over, your balancing point moves
fowards. To keep your balance, you have to move your feet forwards
too. The balancing point of an object is called its centre of gravity .

Perching Parrot

To find out more about the centre of gravify, try making this parrot.

You will need: cardboard, modelling clay, scissors, coloured pencils,
a drawing pencil.

1. Draw a parrot shape on the cardboard. Make sure it has a long tail
which curves under the body, like the one in the picture.
2. Colour in your parrot and cut it out.
3. Put a lump of modelling clay on the end of the tail.
4. Balance your parrot on the end of your finger or on a pencil perch. It
should rock to and fro on its perch. You may have to add or take away
some clay to get the balance just right.

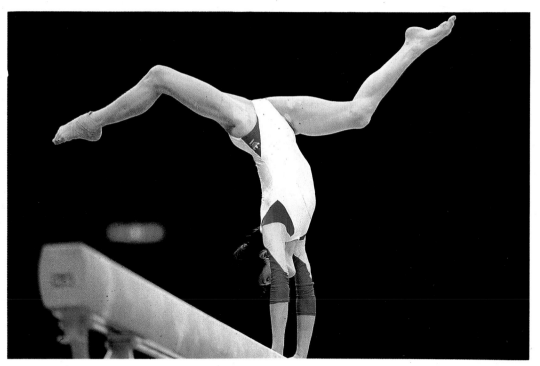

▲ On the balance beam, a gymnast has to keep her centre of gravity right in the middle of her body. Otherwise she will fall off the beam.

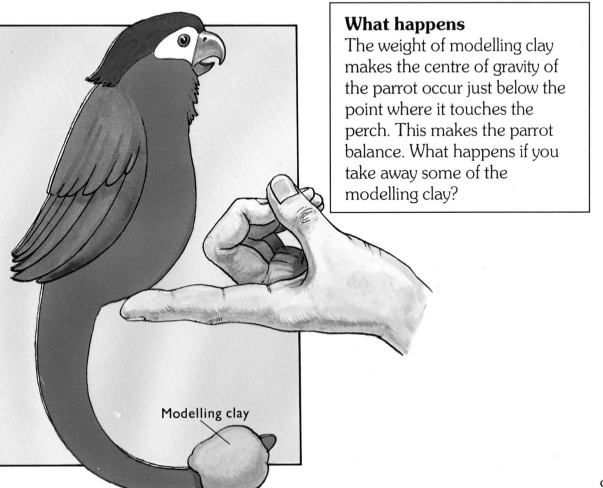

Modelling clay

What happens
The weight of modelling clay makes the centre of gravity of the parrot occur just below the point where it touches the perch. This makes the parrot balance. What happens if you take away some of the modelling clay?

Make a Mobile

A mobile is a balancing act you can make yourself. Moving air pushes it around.

You will need: cardboard, straws, a hole punch, thread, scissors.

1. Draw some shapes on the cardboard and colour them in. Cut out the shapes.
2. Use the hole punch to make a hole in each shape.
3. Cut a small slit in both ends of each straw. It's easier to do this if you flatten the straw before you cut it.
4. Use the thread to tie one shape to each end of one straw.
5. Find the point where the straw hangs level (the balancing point) and tie a thread around the straw at this point.
6. Tie the other end of the thread to one end of a second straw.
7. Tie a shape to the other end of the second straw so that the second straw balances.
8. Keep adding more shapes until your mobile has four layers, which all balance.
9. Hang up your mobile and watch it move. How is a mobile like a see-saw?

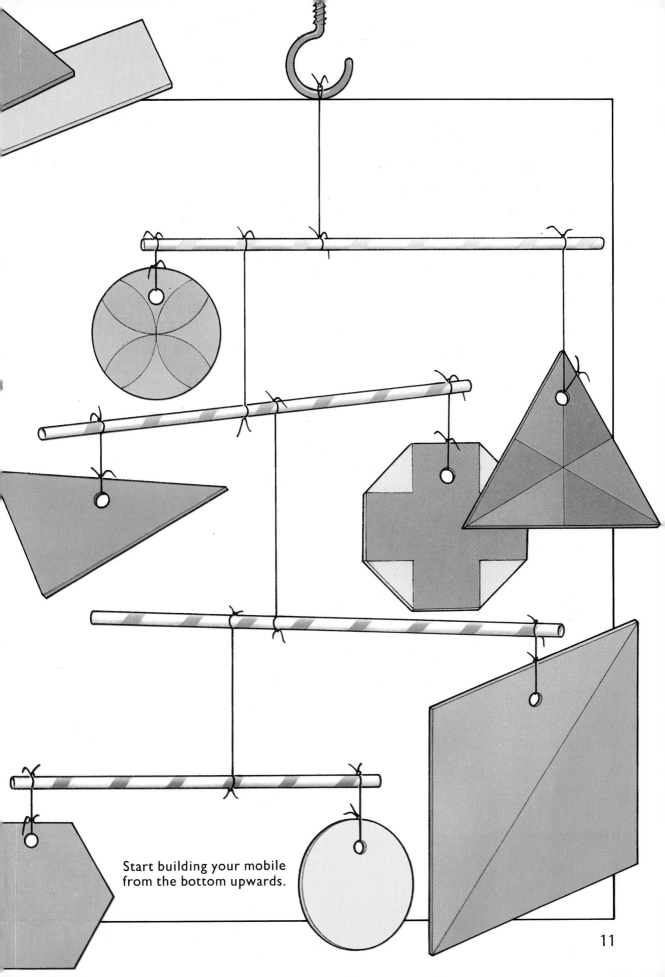

Start building your mobile from the bottom upwards.

WHEELS GO ROUND

Wheels help us to move things along the ground. They are also used to make pots and spin wool. What else are wheels used for?

Wheels and Axles

A wheel on its own is not much use. It needs something to turn on. This is called an axle. Use straws, pencils or thin dowel as axles and cut out wheels from thin card or balsa wood. Use modelling clay to fix the axles to the wheels. You can make the axle and the wheel turn together. Or you can leave the wheel free to turn while the axle stays still.

What happens if the axle is not in the middle of the wheel? Try making different shaped wheels. Which shape turns round most easily?

▲ The wheel is one of the most important inventions ever made. No one knows who invented the wheel but it has been used for thousands of years. This mosaic of a Sumerian cart is nearly 4500 years old.

Make a Land Yacht

You will need:

A small box, 3 or 4 wheels made from card, wood or cotton reels, 2 axles made from straws or dowel, a sail made from paper or cloth and straws or dowel, a mast made from a straw or a garden cane, scissors, glue, modelling clay, cotton thread.

1. Use the scissors to cut two holes near the bottom of one of the long sides of the box. Cut two matching holes on the other side.
2. Push the axles through the holes to match the picture.
3. Use the glue or modelling clay to fix the wheels to the axles.
4. Tie the sail to the mast using the thread.
5. Cut slots in the box to match the picture. Push the mast through the slots and use modelling clay to stand the sail up inside the box.
6. Take your land yacht to a place with a strong wind or roll it down a steep slope. How fast does it move?

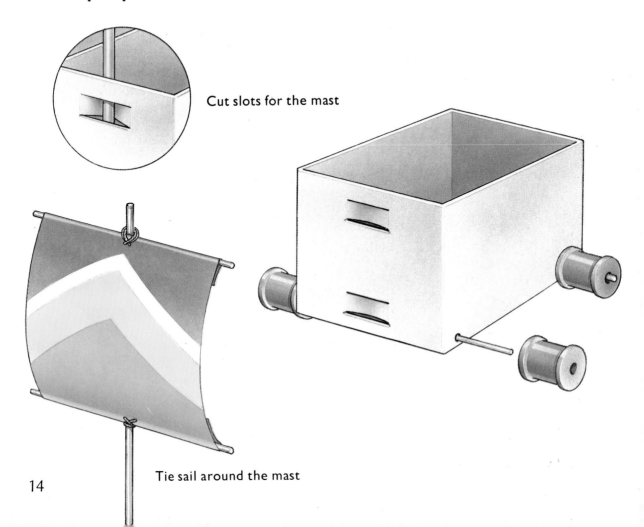

Cut slots for the mast

Tie sail around the mast

You may well have to rig the yacht. Use cotton to tie the sail.

Paint a design on sail.

Modelling clay

Wheels for Measuring

Wheels can be used for measuring distances. Make a measuring wheel yourself. Cut out a circle of card and push a cocktail stick through the middle. Make a mark on the edge of the wheel. Lay your wheel on a piece of paper and use the mark to help you measure the distance the wheel takes to turn round once.

How far do you go for one turn of your bicycle wheel? Ask a friend to help you measure the distance.

Tie a handkerchief around the tyre

◀ Trains run on wheels with a sloping edge, like an ice-cream cone. This shape helps the train to stay on the track. These children are experimenting with different shaped wheels to see which ones are best at staying on the track.

Real train wheels have a special edge called a flange, which helps to keep the engine and coaches from falling off the track.

Wheels for Lifting

A wheel with a groove for carrying a rope is called a pulley. By pulling down on the rope, we can lift heavy things up. Look out for pulleys in cranes, in lifts, on sailing ships and on some washing lines.

You will need: A cotton reel, wire, metal hook, string, a weight such as a brick or a heavy book.

1. Ask an adult to help you fix the hook into a wooden beam.
2. Bend the wire through the cotton reel and make a loop above the reel.
3. Hang the reel over the hook.
4. Tie the string around the weight.
5. Leave the weight on the floor and loop the other end of the string around the cotton reel.
6. When you pull down on the free end of the string, the weight will rise up off the ground. This is much easier than lifting the brick with your bare hands.

Hook

Loop

Cotton reel

Pull

String

Brick

Wheels with Teeth

A wheel with teeth around the edge is called a gear wheel. To make a gear wheel, cut two circles of card. Make a hole through the middle of both circles. Stick pieces of thin wood on to one piece of card. Arrange them in a wheel shape so the end of the wood sticks out around the edge of the circle. Stick the other circle on top.

Circles of card

▼ Gear wheels are used to change the speed or direction of movement. Inside a clock, the gear wheels are arranged so they make the big hand and the little hand turn at different speeds.

To start with, make one big wheel and one small wheel. Push a pencil through the middle of each wheel and push the pencil through a large piece of card. Arrange the gear wheels so the teeth link together.

Turn the big wheel once. Which way does the small wheel turn? How many times does the small wheel turn round? Does the small wheel turn faster or slower than the small wheel?

To make a gear machine, make different sized wheels with different numbers of teeth. Arrange them to match the picture. When you turn one gear wheel, what happens to the other wheels?

STOP AND GO

Have you ever been in a car that stopped suddenly? The sudden force throws you forwards after the car has stopped. A seat belt keeps you in your seat so you don't hit the seats or the windscreen.

You are thrown forwards because of something called inertia. Inertia is a physical property that keeps moving things moving or stationary things still – unless a strong force acts on them. The word inertia comes from the Latin word for laziness.

Flick the Paper

Put a plastic beaker on a piece of paper. Can you pull the paper out from under the mug without knocking it over?

The trick is to pull the paper out very sharply. The mug will be left behind because the pulling force is not strong enough to overcome its inertia. Can you repeat the trick with a mug full of water?

In a Spin

Find two table tennis balls and make a small hole in each one. Make up some jelly and pour the liquid jelly into one of the balls. Leave the jelly to set hard. Pour water into the other ball. Put tape across the holes.

Now spin each ball in turn on a smooth surface. Stop the ball with your fingers and then let go. What happens?

Snapping Strings

Put 500 grammes of small stones or marbles into a small plastic bag. Tie a long piece of thread to the top of the bag and another piece of thread to the bottom of the bag. Rest a stick or broom handle over two chairs and tie the top thread to the stick. Pull the bottom thread sharply. What happens?

Now tie another piece of thread to the bottom of the bag. Pull the bottom thread slowly. What happens this time?

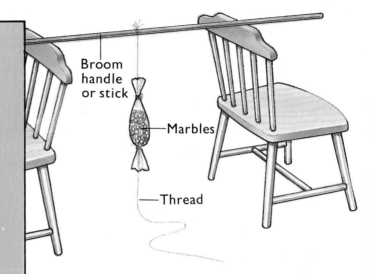

Broom handle or stick

Marbles

Thread

What happens
The water ball will start spinning again when you let go. Inertia keeps the water swirling around inside the ball and this starts the ball spinning again. There is no movement inside the jelly ball. So when you stop it spinning, it stays still. You can use this trick to help you tell the difference between a raw egg and a cooked egg.

What happens
When you pull the bottom thread sharply, the inertia of the stones stops the pull from reaching the top thread. So the bottom thread snaps. When you pull the bottom thread slowly, the steady pull is a strong enough force to overcome the inertia of the stones. This time, the pull reaches the top thread and it snaps first.

STICKING AND SLIPPING

Rub your hands together very quickly. The heat you feel is caused by a force called friction. Friction tries to stop things sliding past each other and slows things down. Without friction, we would slip over every time we tried to walk.

 Science Friction

To find out more about the friction on different surfaces, try these tests.

You will need: a table, string, scissors, a wooden block, a yoghurt pot, marbles, a hook, different surfaces: carpet tiles, sandpaper, shiny hardboard, newspaper.

1. To protect the table, cover it with an old cloth or blanket.
2. Fit the hook into one side of the wooden block.
3. Tie one end of the string to the yoghurt pot and the other end to the hook.

4. Put each surface on to the table in turn.
5. Put the block on top of the surface.
6. To make the block move, how many marbles do you need to put in the yoghurt pot?

Block

Hook

Sandpaper

▲ Skis are very narrow so that only a small surface comes into contact with the snow. They are also smooth underneath. This reduces the amount of friction between the skis and the snow and helps skiers to slide at high speeds over the snow.

Cloth

Weight

What happens

The rough surfaces cause more friction. You need more marbles in the pot to overcome this friction and make the block move. Which surface causes the most friction?

Braking Power

A lot of friction can sometimes be useful. Bicycle brakes work because of friction. When you squeeze the brakes, rubber or plastic pads press against the wheel rims and stop the wheels turning.

Next time you brake hard, stop and feel the wheel rim. It will be warm because of friction.

Too much Friction

Try pushing a book along the carpet. Friction stops the book sliding along easily. Now put some marbles under the book and push it again. This time it moves easily because the marbles roll and cut down the friction.

Sometimes, friction is a problem. In machines, it makes moving parts get hot and wear out more quickly. It also wastes energy. Ball bearings are used to help the moving parts inside machines spin more easily. A bearing is often made of a ring of smooth, shiny balls which roll around in a groove between the fixed and the moving parts of a machine. This reduces friction.

Ball bearings

Make a Hovercraft

A hovercraft floats above the ground or the water on a cushion of air. This cuts down the amount of friction and helps the hovercraft to move more easily.

You will need: a balloon, a polystyrene food tray, a small cork, glue, a knitting needle, modelling clay, a pencil.

1. Ask an adult to use the knitting needle to make a hole through the middle of the cork.
2. Use the pencil to make a small hole in the middle of the food tray.
3. Glue the cork to the bottom of the tray so the holes are lined up.
4. Put modelling clay around the cork to stop air escaping.
5. Put the tray on a smooth surface.
6. Blow up the balloon. Hold the end tightly so the air can't get out and fit the nozzle of the balloon over the cork.
7. Give the tray a gentle push and it should glide away.

What happens

The air from the balloon rushes down through the cork and out under the tray. The air lifts the tray a little way off the floor. When you push your hovercraft, it glides along on this layer of air, just like a real hovercraft.

Tray

Cork

Modelling clay

It is easier to pull a heavy weight up a slope than to lift it straight up. Prove this for yourself. Tie a piece of string around a stone and tie an elastic band to the string. To make a slope, pile up several books and rest a ruler against the books. Use the elastic band to pull the stone up the ruler. How far does the band stretch?

Now take away the ruler and lift the stone straight up from the floor to to the top of the books. Does the elastic band stretch farther this time?

Elastic band
Stone
Ruler

Sliding down Slopes

Tie a piece of string to a heavy object, such as a book or a brick. Pull the string through a bulldog clip. Tie the other end of the string to a handle or fixed bar. Put the bulldog clip at the top of the slope. How long does it take to slide down? Change the angle of the slope. How does this change the speed of the bulldog clip? Try sliding other objects, such as rolls of tape or paper clips, down your slope. How does the size and weight of the object affect its speed down the slope?

Bulldog clip

Rolled-up-Slopes

Screws can be used to lift things, press things or force things apart. A screw holds two pieces of wood together more firmly than a nail.

A screw is really a rolled-up slope. You can check this for yourself. Draw a slope on a piece of paper and cut it out. Then wind the paper around a pencil. Compare this with a real screw.

Did you know that a wedge is two slopes joined back-to-back? An axe is a kind of wedge. If you push a wedge into a gap, you force the load past its sloping sides. This makes it easier to force things apart.

This edge of a screw is called a thread.

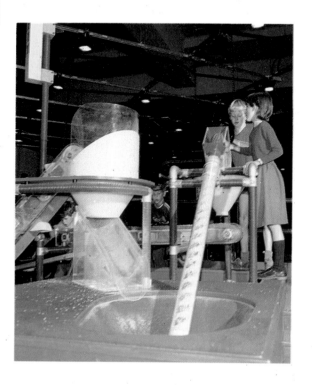

▶ This model of an Archimedes screw is being used to lift grain up out of a pit into a hopper. This machine was invented thousands of years ago by the Greek scientist Archimedes. In Egypt, it is still used to lift water for irrigation.

STRETCH AND TWIST

Pull some of the skin on your arm. How far will your skin stretch? What happens when you let go? Materials that stretch but go back to their original shape are called elastic materials.

Tape

Hair

Tape

Weight

Elastic Materials

Test some different materials to see if they are elastic. Here are some ideas: hair, balloon, wool, cotton, string, plastic, wood.

Tape a small piece of each material to the edge of a table. Measure its length with a ruler. Now stick a weight on the end and measure it again. Does the material stretch? When you take off the weight, does the material go back to its original length?

Make a Weighing Machine

Rubber is an elastic material. You can use an elastic band to make a weighing machine.

You will need: A large piece of cardboard, a pen, a paperclip, strong thread, a yoghurt pot, an elastic band, a strong pin or nail, a ruler.

1. Stick the pin or nail into the card and hang the elastic band from the pin or nail.

2. Open out the paperclip to make a hook shape at one end and a pointer at the other end.

3. Tie one end of the thread or string around the rim of the pot and tie the other end to the paper clip.

4. Put a known weight in the pot and mark the position of the pointer.

5. Put more known weights in the pot, one at a time, until you have made a scale on the cardboard.

6. Use your weighing machine to weigh different objects such as marbles, pencils, stones and paper clips. Make a chart of your results.

Make a Cotton Reel Tank

This tank rolls along using the energy from a twisted elastic band.

You will need: A cotton reel, a small elastic band, three matchsticks, a candle, a ruler, a knife.

Ask an adult to help you with the first three steps.

Hole

Groove

1. Cut a thin slice of wax from the candle.
2. Use the knife to make a hole in the middle of the slice.
3. Make a groove in one side of the slice straight across the middle.
4. Push the elastic band through the hole in the slice and put a matchstick through the band. Pull the band so the matchstick is held in the groove.
5. Pull the other end of the band through the hole in the middle of the cotton reel.
6. Push half a matchstick through the band to hold it in place.
7. Push another matchstick into one of the holes through the reel. This will stop the half matchstick from turning round.
8. To twist the elastic band, turn the matchstick in the groove around several times.
9. When you put your tank on the floor or on a table, the band will slowly unwind and push the tank along.
10. You could have a tank race with your friends.

Bouncing Tests

How high can you make a rubber ball bounce? Draw a scale on a large piece of paper. Drop a ball from different heights and ask a friend to mark how high the ball bounces each time.

Drop several different balls from the same height. Which one bounces the highest? What is this ball made from?

Which sort of surface is best for bouncing? Try grass, soil, wood, sand, cement and carpet.

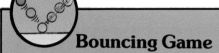

Bouncing Game

Half fill a bucket with sand. Stand three metres away from the bucket. See if you and your friends can get the ball into the bucket with just one bounce. Draw a picture of the path of the bounce. If you stand farther way from the bucket, does the path of the bounce change?

◄ When a ball hits the ground the bottom part of it is squashed and pushed upwards. The ball then springs back into shape, which pushes it up into the air. In the photograph, you can see that the second bounce is lower than the first one.

THE PULL OF THE EARTH

If you throw a ball up in the air, it falls back down to the ground. This happens because of a force called gravity, which pulls things down to the ground. The Earth is so big that the pull of its gravity is very strong. It keeps everything on the Earth. We rely on gravity to pour drinks, post letters or drill holes. Without gravity, everything on Earth would fly off into space.

These astronauts are learning to cope with the 'weightless' feeling they will experience out in Space. On Earth, we have weight because gravity pulls us down to the ground.

Falling Forces

To see how gravity affects falling objects, try these tests.

You will need: newspaper, large sheets of paper, a straw or eyedropper, tape, thin paint or ink.

1. Put lots of newspaper on the floor.
2. Tape a sheet of paper on top of the newspaper.
3. Pick up some of the thin paint or ink with the straw or eyedropper.
4. Drop the paint or ink from a height of 10 centimetres, 30 centimetres, 50 centimetres and 100 centimetres.
5. Before you let each drop fall, guess the size of the blob it will make on the paper.
6. What happens if you drop thicker paint or ink from the same heights?

To make a straw dropper

Hold your finger over the end of a straw. Dip it into the paint or ink. The paint or ink will not fall out until you take your finger off the end of the straw.

What happens

When the paint or ink drops fall from a greater height, gravity makes them fall faster. They are travelling at a faster speed when they hit the ground, so they make bigger marks on the paper.

Anti-gravity Cones

The cones in this investigation seem to roll uphill, against the force of gravity. How is this possible?

1. Cut two pieces of cardboard to match the shape in the picture.
2. Tape the two shortest sides of the card together.
3. Hold the paper by one of the corners on the long side. Make a cone shape by curling the other corner on the long side around your hand. Ask a friend to help you tape the paper to hold it in place.
4. Use scissors to trim the point off the open end of the cone to make a circle.
5. Make another cone exactly the same size and shape. Tape the open ends of the cones together to match the picture.
6. Put the paper cones at the bottom of the hill and watch them climb upwards.

You will need:

Cardboard, plain paper about 20 centimetres by 13 centimetres, a pencil, a ruler, scissors, tape.

What happens

The middle part of the cones really goes downhill. So the cones are not going against the force of gravity. You can prove this by measuring the distance from the middle of the cones to the ground when they are at the top of the hill. At this point, the cones will be lower down than at the bottom of the hill.

Machines need energy to make them work. This power can come from petrol, electricity and the pushing force of water or the wind. Can you think of any other sources of energy for machines?

Make a Windmill

You will need:
A piece of coloured paper about 15 centimetres square, scissors, a pin, a bead, a stick.

1. Cut lines in the piece of paper to match the picture.
2. Fold in the pieces marked with a cross.
3. Push the pin through the middle of the folded pieces.
4. Thread a bead on to the back of the pin.
5. Ask an adult to help you push the pin into a stick.
6. On a windy day, put the windmill outside and see how fast it turns round.

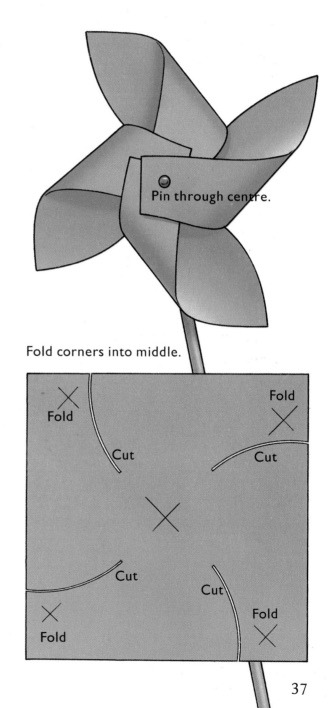

Pin through centre.

Fold corners into middle.

Fold

Fold

Cut

Cut

Fold

Cut

Cut

Fold

Windmills can be used to grind flour or raise water from a well. Nowadays, special windmills are used to make electricity. This does not pollute the environment, but it is only possible in places where there are a lot of strong winds.

37

Cork
Pulley

▼ As this water wheel turns, it lifts water up out of the river and into the irrigation channel.

Knitting needle

Fins

Make a Water Wheel

You will need: A plastic bottle, two corks, small pieces of plastic or thin balsa wood, a knitting needle, scissors, thread, a matchbox.

1. Cut four plastic or wooden fins.
2. Ask an adult to make four slits in the sides of the cork and one hole through the middle of the cork.
3. Push the fins into the slits in the cork.
4. Make a hole in the bottom of the plastic bottle.
5. Push the knitting needle through the cork with the fins, into the bottle and out through the hole in the bottom.
6. Then push the point of the knitting needle into the other cork. The needle should not be able to turn round inside either cork.
7. Hold the bottle, put your water wheel under a tap and watch it turn round.
8. Tie a long thread with a matchbox on the end to the second cork. As the water wheel turns, it will lift up the matchbox. Can you make your water wheel work any other machines?

INDEX

Page numbers in *italics* refer to illustrations or where illustrations and text occur on the same page.

Adviser: Robert Pressling
Designer: Ben White
Editors: Nicola Barber and Annabel Warburg
Picture Research: Elaine Willis

The publishers wish to thank the following artists for contributing to this book:
Peter Bull: page headings, Peter Dennis (Linda Rogers Associates): pp. 8/9, 26–33, 35; Kuo Kang Chen: pp. 4–6, 14–17, 20–25; John Scorey: pp. 10–13, 18/19, 36–39.

The publishers also wish to thank the following for providing photographs for this book:
13 Michael Holford; 4 (*left*) Lesley Howling; 34 NASA; 24 Courtesy, NTN Bearings; 16, 18, 27 Science Museum, London; 32 Science Photo Library; 7, 9, 23 Supersport Photos; 4 (*right*), 38 ZEFA.

Kingfisher Books, Grisewood and Dempsey Ltd, Elsley House, 24–30 Great Titchfield Street, London W1P 7AD

First published in 1990 by Kingfisher Books
10 9 8 7 6 5 4
Copyright © Grisewood and Dempsey Ltd 1990

British Library Cataloguing in Publication Data
Taylor, Barbara
   Machines and Movement.
   1. Materials. Transport
   I. Title   II. Series
   620.1′1

   ISBN 0-86272-529-1

Phototypeset by Southern Positives and Negatives (SPAN), Lingfield, Surrey
Colour Separations by Scantrans pte Ltd, Singapore and Newsele Litho, Milan
Printed in Spain